OPEN YOUR EYES

A Book of Hope

Angie Briggs

WESTBOW
PRESS
A DIVISION OF THOMAS NELSON

ISBN: 978-1-4497-4116-7 (sc)
ISBN: 978-1-4497-4433-5 (e)
Library of Congress Control Number: 2012903204

WestBow Press books may be ordered through booksellers or by contacting:

WestBow Press
A Division of Thomas Nelson
1663 Liberty Drive
Bloomington, IN 47403
www.westbowpress.com
1-(866) 928-1240

Because of the dynamic nature of the Internet, any web addresses or
links contained in this book may have changed since publication and
may no longer be valid. The views expressed in this work are solely those
of the author and do not necessarily reflect the views of the publisher,
and the publisher hereby disclaims any responsibility for them.

Certain stock imagery © Thinkstock.
Any people depicted in stock imagery provided by Thinkstock are models,
and such images are being used for illustrative purposes only.

Author photograph taken by Laura Chism.
Front cover photograph taken by Angie Briggs.

For privacy reasons some names have been changed.

Printed in the United States of America
WestBow Press rev. date: 3/16/2012

This is an expression of gratitude to God for the many miracles He has done in my life.

To my mom for always supporting me and loving me no matter what my circumstances. Thank you for listening and for all the tears and laughs along the way! I love you

To Becky for your ability to speak truth into my life and for your example of faith. Your miracle will be an example to everyone of God's promise keeping. Thank you for believing in me when no one else did. You encouraged me to finish strong and I am forever grateful for your friendship. I am glad to be on the journey with you and I can't wait to see what else the future holds.

To my friends and family for dealing with me during the toughest time of my life and for accepting my "new normal." I know it hasn't been easy. I love you all.To the people mentioned in this book. You are in here for a reason. I learned from you and will be forever changed because of you!

To Don Waddell for your words of encouragement, prayers and last minute editing. Thank you so much!

TABLE OF CONTENTS

THE STORY BEHIND THE STORIES

I am now on my 4th draft of this book and I am praying that I am finally where God wants me to be. I have been arguing, resisting, procrastinating and avoiding the call that God has placed on my life. I was and still am a bit overwhelmed. It seems like such a great responsibility to talk about God and share my personal journey. Although that was never my intention when my journey began, I find myself here now, at a crucial point where I proclaim it to the world how God saved me.

I am writing to you in hopes that you too will **open your eyes** and see that God is everywhere and he wants to guide you and be a part of every aspect of your life. God was not the priority in my life as He is now. It hasn't been an easy journey so I am not going to sugarcoat the fact that it is hard to release control of your life over to someone you can't see. But isn't that what Hope is all about? It's the evidence of things unseen.

If you are a non-believer I get it. I know it's hard to understand how Christians can put their faith in something that is unseen and unexplainable. I claimed to be a Christian even though I still kept God in a pretty nice box and I took him out when I needed him. I didn't want him to tell me how to live or put regulations on the things I wanted to do. I took what I wanted to believe from the Bible and applied it to my life as I wanted. I knew about Jesus but I can't say that I had a personal relationship with him. If I did I probably wouldn't have been living the way I was.

I never even imagined that my life would go the way it has gone in the last 3 ½ years but that's what happens. Life happens. The plans I made for myself failed and I was stuck with nowhere to go. I put my hopes in other people to make me happy or in my dreams to fulfill me. If I made more money I would be happy, if I met Mr. Right I would be happy, if my dad told me he was proud of me then I would be happy. Where does all this come from anyways?

I wonder sometimes why we believe so many lies and live by negative thinking when we have an almighty God who wants to give us hope and peace and joy. Don't you want some of that? I know that it is hard sometimes when life throws you a curveball and it's too big to dodge. My curveball came after I moved home from Orlando and I thought everything was going as I planned. I had plans to move home after being away from my family for about 15 years off and on. I had it all figured out that I would get home, start a business, be around my family for the holidays and meet someone and live happily ever after. Well, the plans I made did happen or so I thought. I moved home, started my business (which has been a dream in my heart ever since I can remember), I was home for all the holidays and I got to fall in love with a wonderful guy. I thought life couldn't get any better.

I was still doing things the way I always did them and I didn't realize how lost I was until things started to fall apart. When I lost my dad to a heart attack in January of 2008 it was only the beginning of the pieces of my heart starting to crumble. About five months later my boyfriend who I was madly in love with and wanted to share my life with died. While going through the grieving stages of both of them the economy tanked and I almost had to close down my business. It was too much to handle but I am thankful that God found me when he did.

I want you to know that even when you don't feel like God is anywhere near you, let me reassure you that he is. He is always working behind the scenes but you have to look up and open your eyes to see him. He won't make you love him. He gives us that choice even though his love never changes.

I know sometimes things don't happen the way we think they should. There's a lot of injustice in the world and we lose our loved ones even when we pray so much. I can't explain all of that because I have no idea myself. All I know is that God has a plan for all of us. He is the one who created us so he can give and he can take away. It's hard for us to surrender to that theory because we are such a "me" driven society. If things don't go our way then we just try something different. If we don't feel like we are "in love" with our spouses we just throw them out and get a new one and go into the same problems as before. We don't want to hear the truth and face our fears so things get hidden in the deep recesses of our hearts.

Why do we live like that? Don't you want peace? Don't you want hope?

Ultimately I think the answer is yes for everyone but we try to get it ourselves. God is the only one who can provide that for you, for me. It's not money, it's not sex, drugs, alcohol or materials or even another person. But until we figure that out we will be lost and on our own.

I heard the phrase that God is a jealous God and I never understood what it meant until everything in my life was threatened and most was taken away from me. Would God be enough for me when my dad wasn't there for me to get his approval, advice or safe fatherly love? Would God be enough for me when the person I had been praying for all my life was taken away from me before his time? Would God be enough for me if my business failed and I had no money?

I found out my answer was yes and my journey began in 2008. Truthfully, it wasn't easy. There were times when I questioned what I was doing or how I could go on. There were times when I wanted to give up and leave this world. Sometimes the hurt came from those closest to me because my life was changing and I didn't know how to explain what was going on inside of me and that was terrifying. All along though I knew that God was protecting me and I can't give you a tangible explanation for that. I just knew it. I am grateful that God never gave up on me. Other people did, some of my friends did, some of my family did, but God didn't. He knew what I had in me and he gave me the strength to come up out of the deep waters and let my light shine.

In 2008 God showed up after a long night of grieving the loss of my boyfriend. I cried out to him and the next morning he answered. It was the moment my eyes were opened and I knew he heard me.

I hope that through these short stories you will see that God works through music, friends, church, nature, circumstances and of course, the written word, the Bible. For me he had to work though everything else before I could get to the Bible so do not feel bad if you've never picked one up. You will need to eventually because it really does breathe life into your spirit but remember that this is a journey and we are all learning. We learn and receive in different ways and we go to different churches and should respect that fact. The most important thing is that you start the journey with God, make time to get to know Jesus and understand what he did for you when he died on the cross. Let Jesus into your heart and trust him with your life, all of it.

Once you do you will find a peace that transcends all understanding even when things may be a little rough. You will have strength when others view you as weak. You will have HOPE when you have experienced God's love for you and once you have that you will have FAITH and faith can move mountains!

To God be the Glory,

Angie

Romans 8:24-25 (NIV)

[24] *For in this hope we were saved. But hope that is seen is no hope at all. Who hopes for what they already have?* [25] *But if we hope for what we do not yet have, we wait for it patiently.*

BOOK 1- GOD IS ALWAYS WORKING BEHIND THE SCENES

Encounter with an Angel?

I can still remember this day like it was yesterday. I am a believer that there are angels here on earth to help us so I have always been baffled by an encounter I had when I was working at a small skin care clinic in Indiana in 1998.

A lady came in to get a facial and it was (to my knowledge) her first time in as a client. I remember having a conversation about the five love languages during her facial and she was telling me that we all express love in different ways. I think I was having problems with my boyfriend at the time, that I was living with, so she was trying to help me. We didn't talk about religion but I believe God was mentioned a few times. She was just a very pleasant person and I was glad she came in.

The massage therapist who was working with me that

day was standing at the front desk when she checked out. We chatted for a few more minutes and said our goodbyes. When she walked out the door she turned her head and gave me a smile that I will never forget. It's hard for me to describe but the way her eyes looked back at me and the way she smiled went right through my whole body. It was like she was trying to tell me something but I couldn't understand what I was feeling.

After she went down the stairs, my co-worker and I looked at each other. She noticed it too. She looked at me and said, "Whoa, what was that all about? Did you see the way she looked at you?" "Yea, that was weird huh?"

I had another appointment to get ready for so I couldn't ponder it for too long. I went in to my next service a little baffled but I quickly forgot about it and focused on my next client.

When I came out to the desk after about an hour or so I saw a gift bag on the desk. My co-worker said that the lady who just left brought it back for me. In it was a white Bible with my name engraved on it.

"Wow, how could she get that done so fast? That is so nice." Again we both looked at each other like something bigger was going on. My co-worker said "I wonder if she is an angel." "I was thinking the same thing. It was just too weird and how did she get that done so fast? And the smile she gave me?"

Why would we both think that? I guess you just had to be there to experience what we saw.

I was finished with my day so I went back to the phone book to get her address. I was going to send a thank you card and also put her on our mailing list. This was back when you had to look up everything in the phone book.

I checked her name and there was a phone number but no address. I called and there was no answer, no answering machine, nothing. I tried a few more times the rest of the week, but still nothing.

I had an excited feeling in my spirit but I didn't know what to do with it. I wasn't sure what had just happened but I knew it was something special.

I believe God sent that person in to me for some divine purpose that I may never know. I still have that Bible and I think of her every time I pick it up. What was her mission? Why me? Why then?

I wasn't on a real spiritual journey at that point in my life. I was living with my boyfriend and not even going to church on a regular basis but I liked talking about God. I went home and told my boyfriend that I thought I met an angel and he looked at me like I was crazy. I didn't care. I knew that I experienced something different and I wasn't going to let him take away from my excitement.

Still, something inside of me has joy and peace when I think about my angel encounter. I can remember her face clearly to this day.

It would be 11 more years before I gave my life to Christ but God was already working on me.

> *What I learned about God: He was watching out for me long before I knew it*

As I look back on that day it makes me realize that God still cared about me even when I was making wrong decisions. He was patiently waiting for me and it makes me feel like he was watching out for me. He sent someone in to give me a Bible. That should have been a pretty clear message to me but after the wonder of the story I went right back to living the way I was living. It was a great story but I didn't necessarily apply it to my life at the time. He was trying to send me a message but I guess I wasn't ready to hear it. I continued to live in sin and stayed in an unhealthy relationship because I didn't want to be by myself. I'm so thankful God had his eye on me.

Hebrews 1:14 (NIV)

Are not all angels ministering spirits sent to serve those who will inherit salvation?

BOOK 2- THE DAY MY EYES WERE OPENED

A Sign from Heaven

September 13, 2008. It was still summer technically but it felt more fall-like this morning. It was a regular day by most people's standards. I got up, took a shower, put some make-up on and tried to look halfway decent. I had no appointments on the book at my skin care studio but I had to go to work. What else was I going to do? Stay home and cry all day? I had already been up all night doing that so my eyes were tired and puffy. I don't even know if I could have produced any more tears anyways. The grief came over me the night before like a freight train and thankfully my best friend was kind enough to just listen to me for a little while. She was struggling to find words to console me so she just stayed on the phone with me and listened. She had lost her dad a few years ago so she understood that pain and loss but she was in unchartered territory on the death of my 37 year old boyfriend whom she had met as well.

Leslie has been married for a long time but since we go back about 20 years she knew how much I wanted someone special in my life. Her and her husband had been with me through several boyfriends and break-ups over the years and they thought, like me, that I had finally met the right one.

"I just want to know that God can hear me."

I told Leslie that I have been praying all the time talking to God, crying to him, desperate to feel something. I needed something but I wasn't sure what it was. I was ok when I was at work because giving a facial to someone was helping my sanity. I was thankful that I had my business to concentrate on and people who were counting on me to help them feel better. Somehow talking about how you are supposed to clean your skin and get rid of cellulite was good therapy for me. Since I had just started my business the clients I did have were a huge blessing. In fact I think God gave me a few busy months just to help me get through it. For a short time it took my mind off of what happened and how hopeless I was.

Leslie reminded me of a prayer she said when she was trying to make a decision about something and she just prayed simply "God if you are here I need a sign."

We hung up the phone and I brought Sammy, my dog, in closer to me. I needed that unconditional love that a pet brings in times of sorrow. He looked as if he knew exactly what I needed. His brown eyes, so full of expression, let me know he was well aware of my sadness. He got up really close to my eyes and started licking my tears away which brought a smile to my face. More tears followed because I was so grateful to have him and my two cats there with me. I wasn't alone after all.

It was as if he was saying "It's going to be ok mom, I love you." Duke, my male cat quickly followed Sammy's actions but he liked licking my eyelashes for some reason. Daisee didn't care too much for group therapy. I knew she would come in later and snuggle with me when she was ready.

I was amazed at how these precious little creatures offered me more in that moment than any human could have.

As I lay in bed I just opened my heart up to God and talked with Him for a little while. It seemed so surreal, like I was the only one on the planet pleading with God Almighty. Did I have to remind him that I was down here suffering the loss of my boyfriend and five months before that my dad died? Did he remember that all this happened to me? Did he remember that my boyfriend and I just met and were in love? Did he remember that I have been praying to meet him my whole life or that I wanted my dad to walk me down the aisle and see me finally happy with someone? Did he know that this wasn't part of the plan, my plan?

I needed God, where was He?

I did what my friend suggested and prayed in a way that was different than before. I was humbled at how I couldn't do anything to fix this problem. I couldn't run away or move to a different state and make it go away. Here it was; harsh, cold reality and I had to face it. I was tired, defeated and desperate for someone to hold me and tell me it was going to be ok. I was all alone and afraid of what my future held. I lost hope in the one thing I thought I just found, true love.

"I need you God. Please give me a sign that you are here with me."

Duke was lying on top of my head but somehow I managed to turn on my side, pull Sammy in close and cry myself to sleep.

Morning came and it was hard to face another day but I had no choice. I was still here and I had my new business to run. I lived at my brother's rental house about a ½ mile away from my shop. Sammy and I walked all around that neighborhood usually but not in the mornings. I have never been one to get up at the crack of dawn and exercise or anything like that so mornings for him were for relieving himself and that's it. On the weekends and evenings we took long walks or went to my mom's to hang out. He loves his Granny.

We went across the street to the "Moses Bush" as I used

to call it. It was a tree-like bush that stood by itself that Sammy liked to pee on. Every time I saw that bush I pictured God speaking to Moses through it and it would be burning by itself. Of course, this thought would only last a second. I didn't ponder over it or anything. It was just a random weird thought.

While Sam would do his business I would usually check out the morning sky and see what kind of day was before me. This particular morning was beautiful and the sun was shining. There were some clouds in the sky but it was not overcast. It was one of those mornings that felt really peaceful and it was very quiet. It was only 9am on a Saturday so there wasn't much going on.

I looked up to check out the sky and did a double take. A huge cross was hovering directly over me and I stopped and stared at how beautiful it was. I walked all around the block looking at it from different angles making sure it wasn't an "x" as if somehow that would change everything if it were slightly off but it wasn't, it was a cross. I hadn't heard any planes flying overhead prior to seeing it but I can't say that there were no planes either. It just stayed around for so long it baffled me a bit. After I got over the practical explanation I reveled in its size and beauty and couldn't help but remember that I prayed for a sign and there it was.

I don't know how to describe what I felt but silently,

in the deepest part of my heart, I heard God say at that very moment "I'm here, I can hear you." I felt a peace that day that everything was going to be okay, that I wasn't alone.

I called Leslie and told her that I was standing under the biggest cross I have ever seen. "I got my sign." "Take a picture of it and email it to me when you get to work, I can't wait to see it."

"Ok.duh, I didn't even think about taking a picture."

I quickly went back to the house and fumbled around to find my digital camera. My cell phone took horrible pictures. I was hoping it wouldn't fade before I got back even though I was only a minute away. It didn't fade. It stayed around and I took several pictures from all the different angles. I was amazed and very thankful God did that for me. There was no question that cross was for me. I knew it in my heart.

I emailed it to Leslie when I got to work. "If you don't take that as a sign Angie, you've got a serious issue." We both laughed. I knew it was my sign.

That day changed my prayer and thought life forever.

It was the moment my eyes were opened to a God who was waiting to save me.

What I learned about God: God is everywhere

After I saw the cross in the sky I started to notice God in everything I did. I can't really explain it but something was different. I just felt that if God did that for me and if he could hear my prayers then I needed to watch my thoughts and pray more often. Even though I thought I had a pretty good relationship with Him I could feel that He was trying to talk to me.

God didn't waste time after the cross in the sky. One of the first things He changed was what I was listening to everyday on the radio. My friend had been listening to a Christian radio station while we were on our way to a baseball game and I noticed her daughter singing along to one of the songs. "What are you listening to?" I asked. "Oh, it's an awesome Christian station. You should check it out. I think you'll like it." We had pretty similar tastes in music so I opened my mind and listened. It was great but I didn't think I would be listening to it all the time or anything. I did tune my radio to it on the way home. I cried the whole way home.

I tried to turn the station back to my country music but it didn't last long. God was using music to speak to me in a big way.

<u>Psalms 34:18 (NIV)</u> *"God is close to the brokenhearted and saves those who are crushed in spirit."*

BOOK 3- A PLACE WHERE I BELONG

CHAPTER 1

When I went back to working at my shop I felt pretty useless. Since I had just started my skin care business in late 2007 I was still building my clientele. I have to say that the fact that I love my job really helped me get through the first month and ½ after my boyfriend passed away and it gave me a purpose to get up out of bed. I didn't have anyone helping with the bills so I didn't have a choice. It's a little foggy that whole month of July and even August. I went to church a few times with his family and I was trying to find a church home but was not feeling right anywhere in particular.

Leslie invited me to go to church at Southeast Christian which is a mega church here in Louisville. I actually used to make fun of this church quite often which doesn't say much about me as a person but I am just being honest. I just didn't get it. I would say the same things that people now say to me like "it's a cult, or "so, you're drinking the kool-aid too, huh?" I was safe and comfortable in my Catholic shoes and I wasn't even thinking about changing. I agreed to go with her one Sunday.

When I walked into Southeast I felt a lot of energy and there were a ton of people bustling around. The place is huge. I thought I was going to a concert and I was anxiously anticipating what was to come. When we walked in they were singing one of the songs I heard on the Christian radio station. That was great and it was pretty loud and everyone was singing. This was a good thing since I love to sing but God skipped the gift giving for me in that area. I am a little tone deaf.

God obviously knew I would like it there because of the big crowd and the great music but I'm sure there was more to his plan. It was a little uncomfortable at first since I was so used to going to mass and following the traditional Catholic rituals. I wasn't too sure about how they did communion and no one else was doing the sign of the cross. That was weird for me. I did it anyways because that's what I was used to and I wasn't going to change just because I was in a new church. That's the stubborn in me coming out.

The pastor came out and he was young and funny and gave a good sermon. There may have been a baptism, I don't recall. I was in a new world, my new world but I had no clue what God was doing or how he was working things out. Leslie was making sure I was doing ok and asked me if I liked it and I told her yes but I wasn't sure if I would be going all the time or not. I still had it in my head that I was going to find a nice Catholic church. I went to the church where I grew up with my mom the next Sunday and for a couple of weeks I went to both services just to see where I wanted to be. I guess I was craving community or something. I knew I needed something but I wasn't sure what it was.

As I would sing songs of praise at my new church I couldn't help but have tears streaming down my face. How could I get through these songs when I didn't feel thankful? I was sad and even angry that I had to go through the loss of my dad and my boyfriend and I just couldn't comprehend songs like "It is well with my soul" and "Amazing Grace." It was the beginning of my journey and it would be a long time before I could even grasp the concept of praise and worship. Plus, we didn't call it that at my church so there was a lot of changing going on and I wasn't sure about any of it.

After I had been attending Southeast for about four months or so I started to feel a little nudge about joining the church. At the end of every service they would say "If you've never made a decision for Christ to be your Lord and Savior, you can come down front and make that decision today or if you would like to make this church your home you can come down front as we stand and sing." I had seen countless people doing this, but I was definitely not used to this kind of thing. My decisions were made for me by my parents. I was raised Catholic. I am grateful for the fact that my parents had faith and brought me up the way they did. I had just never been to a nondenominational Christian church.

I believed in Jesus Christ, that he rose from the dead and that he is the son of God. No questions, no doubts. I didn't believe that it was just some great story. I believed it happened, every bit of it. I don't think I grasped the concept of what Jesus did exactly for me on that cross, until recently. I didn't grasp the concept of sins being forgiven and forgotten. I still held onto guilt of my sins because people say they forgive but they don't forget, whereas God when he forgives its forgotten when you're a believer and you repent. It took me a while to get this idea. So don't be discouraged if you don't understand yet. Actually, I don't think we will ever be able to fully comprehend exactly what Jesus did for us but if we keep seeking him, slowly but surely, he will reveal what that kind of love looks like.

"What is happening to me?" I knew I was changing but I had never experienced what I was feeling each time I went to a service there. I felt at home and at ease. I felt like I belonged.

Most people seemed like they enjoyed being there and I noticed that no one left early. People stayed for a little while afterward to meet with each other and have coffee so I liked the social aspect of it too.

I had a pretty heightened awareness of baptisms at this point and every time I witnessed one at church I felt the same thing: that nudge you can't explain, the slight shaking and the voice you can hear in your heart of hearts. I knew I had to do it. I had to go forward. I wasn't sure what that really entailed but I soon would find out.

Chapter 2 – Baby steps right?

I got the courage up and went forward one Sunday morning. It was very emotional and exciting but I was nervous. This was all new to me and I was stepping out in a big way from my Catholic traditions. What would my family think? How are they going to take the news that I am now going to be a member at Six Flags over Jesus? That's the nickname that people have for Southeast here in Louisville. It makes me sad that I used to be one of them. But things change and people can to. I made fun of a church without even stepping foot in the door. I wondered why I did that. The worst thing about it was that when I was making fun of them I wasn't even going to church myself. I was saying that I was a Christian but only when it was convenient.

I went back to the room where they meet people who

want to be members and got introduced to a nice lady. She went over a new member booklet and made sure I was on the same page as the church with my beliefs. She asked me if I had been baptized and I said "Yes, as a baby. " I told her I was brought up Catholic. She went on to say that to become a member you had to be baptized by immersion, which means underwater.

I got a little restless. "So it doesn't count that I've been baptized as a baby? " I could feel my blood rising but I wasn't sure why I was getting angry. At this point, I just wanted to join the church. I knew God wanted me to join but I didn't know all this was coming with it.

I asked to speak with the head pastor and he came right over and was very friendly.

"What brought you to Southeast?"

"My best friend invited me. I was looking for a church home. My boyfriend just died in June and five months before I lost my dad."

"I'm so sorry." He said some nice words, of course, and then said "so you have some questions about baptism?"

"Yes, I don't understand why I have to be baptized when I already have been as a baby."

"I understand, about 30% of our members were brought up Catholic so you're not alone. Do you feel that by being baptized, you're betraying your parent's decision?"

"Yes, I guess that's what is".

He went on to explain that this was going to be my decision to follow Christ and make him my Lord and Savior and that I should be grateful for my parents decision of faith to baptize me as a baby. This was just an extension of what they started. He suggested that I watch the DVD on baptism, read over the material, pray about it and if I had any questions to please ask.

I felt very thankful for him taking the time to explain that to me. I still wasn't sure what I was going to do but it definitely helped.

A weird thing happened when I left there. I'm not sure if I didn't hear correctly that you can't be a member until you're baptized by immersion or if I just didn't want to hear it. I could continue to go to church there as long as I wanted. In fact the lady told me that there were many people that have been going there for years and still haven't joined the church. It was nice to not be pressured to join. It was totally my decision.

The pressure wasn't coming from them it was coming from God. He wanted me at this church for some reason and I knew I had to do it. I also knew he wanted me to get baptized but I was just so confused on why.

I went over to the fitness center at the church a few days after walking forward because I was ready to utilize the facilities. They have a huge fitness center that is free to members so I thought that was great. I filled out the paperwork and turned it in to get my ID card and the guy at the desk said I couldn't get it processed fully because I hadn't completed the required steps. "What? " I was frustrated that I had to go through this again and explain that I had been baptized as a baby. He said I could still come to the gym as a guest, but I wouldn't be a regular member until I completed all the steps. I stomped out of there. I was very frustrated and actually almost considered not going back to church. What the heck, I don't get it. Why do I have to be immersed? It was like everything the pastor said went right out the window. I called my new friend Becky who, among others, God sent right at the nick of time to walk alongside me on this journey. She was brought up Catholic too and had just joined the church a few months before. She and I met right after my boyfriend passed away when she came in to get a facial at my shop. We connected instantly and have been friends ever since. She has a way of explaining things, is wise beyond her years and has a strong faith. She had just recently made a decision to get baptized as well.

"Why am I angry about this?" I asked during the phone conversation.

"I don't know do you think its anger or fear? "

"I have no idea. It's not like God is asking me to do something horrible, he is asking me to follow Christ. Why would I be angry?" She explained that the Holy Spirit was convicting me and the resistance I felt was coming on because I knew what I was supposed to do and wasn't doing it.

Well that makes sense but I still wasn't sure. So I went on about my days as usual for about a month after walking forward. God was still talking to me though. At the gym they had Scriptures painted on the walls as I walked around the track. I would read constantly the Scripture from Luke 12:8 "I tell you, whoever acknowledges me before men the Son of Man will also knowledge him before the Angels of God." I knew in my heart that this is what God wanted me to do. I don't think I really understood fully what exactly I was doing. I just knew that baptism was my next step.

I wasn't sure how my family was going to take the news so I started with my mom and then went down the line to my siblings. No one understood why I had to do this and I was such a new baby Christian I had no clue how to explain it. I just said, "It's what I'm supposed to do." I think my siblings were scared I was going to turn into some coo-coo Christian or something so we just avoided talking about it altogether.

Chapter 3–Going Under

My mind was made up and my heart was ready. I was listening to Christian music pretty much all the time by this point and the words to some of the songs were spot on and described exactly what was happening in my life. It was amazing how this music was changing my life. At this point I wasn't spending time in the Bible so this was my time with God.

I decided that March 1, 2009 would be a day for new beginnings. A new chapter for Angie; I'm committing my life to Jesus. Wow, have things changed. Leslie and her husband Terry joined me in baptism that day and it was a day I'll never forget. We have known each other for a long time and have been through a lot together so to have them there sharing that experience was amazing. My mom was the only one that came from my family, but that was okay. I had a couple friends come to support my decision and it was a very happy day. My mom still didn't understand what exactly I was doing but she wanted to be there for me.

When I stepped out into the water it was as if no one in the huge sanctuary was even there. Here I was declaring publicly to a couple thousand people but it was as if it were just me and God in the water, as if I had an audience of one. He told me to do this and I obeyed. My stubborn, strong willed, very mental self, had surrendered to someone for the first time ever.

What I learned about God: He wants total commitment

This was the beginning of the very upside down way of Jesus entering into my life. I guess deep down, I thought that after I got baptized everything was going to be easier and would immediately get better. I didn't realize God had to make major changes in all areas of my life to get me in the space he needed me to be. To be able to be more like Jesus I had to have a lot of things cleaned up in my life. I was in for a long ride, but I never knew that with all these changes, I would get to experience and understand God's grace and peace to get through them. Of course, I didn't expect it to get as bad as it got.

Another thing I didn't realize was that when **you give your life to Christ you can no longer live the way you used to and get away with it.** It doesn't mean you have to be perfect because I tried that too. It just means that God wants to be in all areas of your life and sometimes He may need to clean out some clutter.

2 Corinthians 5:17 (NIV)

Therefore, if anyone is in Christ, the new creation has come: The old has gone, the new is here!

BOOK 4- STUCK IN THE MUCK

CHAPTER 1-

My days were pretty typical and I was trying to stay busy and focused on my business. It was difficult to go out with friends because it reminded me of how lonely I was. Everyone around me was either married or had just started dating someone. It was a constant reminder of the plans I once had for my life that failed and a pain in my heart that was so deep it was hard to explain. I felt like a shell of a person walking around. I wanted everyone to know my pain and feel sorry for me. I felt guilty that I was still here and able to see my dreams come true and my boyfriend couldn't do that.

I felt bad for my mom because she didn't have dad anymore. Even though they did fight and bicker that was just the way they did things. I still knew that my dad loved my mom and vice versa.

I hung out with my boyfriend's family and we managed to get even closer than before. I think we needed each other because it reminded us of him but it grew increasingly difficult for me and I'm sure for them. I struggled with the fact that I thought I had to replace him. My life would eventually move on and I would eventually have to meet someone else. What would that do to his title? He was my perfect boyfriend and I wanted him to stay that way.

With all this going on inside of me it was hard to concentrate on growing my business. It's like all my confidence went out the window. I felt defeated in all areas. I was scared that my business would be next, like I was waiting for the other shoe to drop. The economy had just taken a plunge right when my business opened so the future didn't look bright. I felt more alone than ever. I thought my dad would always be there to give me advice and Josh would be there to support me.

It started becoming clear that my debt was reaching astronomical proportions and there wasn't enough revenue to make some payments to my credit cards or even order products for my services. The financial pressure began to mount and creditors began calling to get their money. I managed to make it through each time but was still making the wrong decisions. I was robbing Peter to pay Paul and so on. This was my life now but I was somehow managing it. I guess I was used to living in chaos so I thought it was normal. This was not something new. I had never been really smart in the finance arena. I got by and made a few smart financial decisions in my lifetime but not many.

Chapter 2- A hot mess

My mom was getting worried about me. She could see the amount of pressure I was under financially and I'm sure felt awful. The creditors were calling her house all the time because I used to live there. She offered to loan me more money but I had to say no because it was getting out of hand. I got myself into this mess and I had to get out of it.

She saw that I was going to church and had met some new Christian friends but my situation looked like it was getting worse. She started to worry that I was going to lose it mentally I think. I kept reassuring her that I would not ever do anything to myself. I knew that's what she was thinking. I even asked her that. She said she was just worried but I could tell.

I will have to admit that there was a time and I think it was only once that things got so bad and I just felt so much pressure of everything combined that I thought "it would be a lot easier to just die, I mean how much more can one person take?" I knew that I would never do anything to hurt myself and I was surprised that I even had that thought. I quickly thought of all the hurt that I would cause to my family and I just needed to somehow get through it. There had to be a light somewhere in the future, right?

Right about the same time as all this was happening,

I was still attending church and still singing songs that were hard to get through.

I can see a light that is coming to the heart that holds on, there will be an end to these troubles but until that day comes, still I will PRAISE you, still I will PRAISE you.

I remember being so overwhelmed with emotion one time that I almost fell to the ground. I sang that song with so many tears in my eyes. And then shortly after that day I heard this message at a Bible study (not sure who said it).

We have to lose something; if we do not grow weary it will come. Sow the seeds in tears, keep taking God at his word and you will reap the harvest.

I have this written in my Bible because I need to read it all the time.

"Yeah, well this is a lot to go through and you keep talking about a harvest God and I don't even see how it is going to happen." I was getting angry with God. I thought after I gave my life to Him things would be easier and this was brutal. I had already lost my dad, my boyfriend and now I may lose my business.

I noticed other people who had lots of material things, a husband and a family, nice clothes, not that much stress, but no faith, no God. How was this possible? I have faith, just turned my life over to Christ, have no money, no food, worn out clothes, no customers, no money, no boyfriend (in fact the one I had died), **no hope.**

This is not fair.

How am I going to shine my light that church keeps talking about? How are other people going to want to come to this church at my suggestion when they look at my life and see it falling apart? If I feel so defeated, how am I going to help anyone?

One thing I've always said and I'm sure other people have this thought is "how come I never knew I was this messed up?" I mean I didn't have this many problems before. Everything was going fine. I had a nice, cushy job, 3 pets, owned my own condo, lived in Florida and had a great social life. Can't I just go back to my old life?

What I learned about God: He will give you strength and courage to climb the mountain

Since everything was crashing down at the same time I felt like I couldn't see a way out. There are different stages of grief you have to go through in order to heal so that was piled on top of financial difficulty. I knew that some things were out of my control but the things I could control were already so messed up that I couldn't fathom it lessening. It was hard to get through those songs of praise but I did it. It hurt then but I think it's what saved me in the long run. God knew my hurts, my disappointments and even my sin that created the messes yet He still gave me the strength and grace I needed to get though it all.

It also taught me about how powerful God is. He can give us life and He can take it away too. I was humbled and overwhelmed at how He cared for me but also how He didn't want me to continue living the way I was living and continue to increase my debt. This was a long process for me to get through because I had lived on credit cards for so long and spent money I didn't have. I got in over my head and didn't even think about it until my world came crashing down. It just so happened, that for me, I was dealing with grief at the same time. I don't know how I would have made it without God in my life.

Galatians 5:1 (NIV)

[1] *It is for freedom that Christ has set us free. Stand firm, then, and do not let yourselves be burdened again by a yoke of slavery.*

BOOK 5- SOMEONE TO WALK ALONGSIDE ME

CHAPTER 1

I had become friends with another small business woman through a local chamber event and thankfully (I hate saying that but I know God put us together for a reason) she was going through the same financial struggles in her small business with just different circumstances. Her and I became really close and are still great friends today.

We used to talk about creditors calling and how our businesses were struggling. We tried to promote each other's business and refer people back and forth.

She had a daily devotional she would read by Joyce Meyer and would share the passages with me when she could. It was nice to meet another Christian woman going through similar financial struggles. God used our friendship to keep us on the right path. When she was up I was down, when I was up she was down.

When I was living at my brother's house things were

extremely tight and I didn't have money to go to the grocery store very often. I lived on cans of tuna, peanut butter and salsa and crackers. My family would never allow me to go hungry but I didn't want to tell them how bad it really was. We usually got together as a family on Sundays so I would take leftovers and make it last as long as possible.

I was in way over my head but had too much pride to ask for help. I had already borrowed money from my brother and my mom so I didn't want to go there anymore.

One day I was getting ready for work and I looked in the cabinets to see if I had anything to take to work that day for lunch. There was nothing and I had no money that week for groceries. I cried and thought to myself "I have no idea how I am going to get food."

I had plans on visiting my friend for an hour or so that day so I called to let her know I was on my way. "Come on over sweetie, I've got something for you too."

We visited for awhile and I used her exercise facility and steam room. She read the daily devotional by Joyce and then she said "Here you go, I picked up some things for you at Wal-mart Grocery."

"What's this? You're buying me groceries now?" We both chuckled but she went on to tell me that she heard God's voice so loudly when she was at Wal-mart, that she was supposed to buy me some groceries. She said she was like "ok, how is she going to react to that?" we hadn't known each other for very long. God said again "get Angie some groceries" she said "ok, what should I get her?" He got very specific and told her to get chicken breasts, asparagus, oatmeal and bananas. I think that's all that was in there. There may have been some squash. I could tell she was nervous about giving me the groceries.

"Thank you so much, I don't know what to say."

I thought to myself, "I have never had anyone get me groceries before." We both just smiled and hugged. No words were needed at that point.

I went out to my car and just started crying. I waited until I left her parking lot because I knew she didn't want to embarrass me. It must have been difficult for her to do that. I wasn't angry. I was so grateful that God cared about me so much. He knew I had too much pride to ask anyone for help so he sent help to me. I was overwhelmed with emotions. God was providing for me in so many ways. I was definitely not starving, I was not in poverty, technically, but I was going down, quickly. I am so grateful for all the family dinners I had that literally happened exactly when I needed them. I felt so guilty because I had nothing to contribute. I couldn't help someone if I wanted to.

What I learned about God: He will provide for you

When I look back at all the times I barely made it in many circumstances I can see God's hand in everything. I never went hungry. I was scared but things always worked out in the long run. I don't wish those days on anyone. It was a very humbling time for me and I'm not real happy about some of the choices I made that got me into the mess I was in. The good thing is that as soon as I started trusting in God the best I knew how, he made a way. Time and time again He came through for me. Most of the time it was at the very last minute but what I realize now is that He was keeping me solely dependent upon him and strengthening my faith with each trial.

Isaiah 58:11 (NIV)

[11] *The LORD will guide you always; he will satisfy your needs in a sun-scorched land and will strengthen your frame. You will be like a well-watered garden, like a spring whose waters never fail.*

CHAPTER 2– A FRIDAY NIGHT AT THE FITNESS CENTER

It had been a long day at work but not because I had a ton of customers. Actually, when God wants to speak to me loudly He usually wipes out my book so I will have time to process everything. Of course, I only know this because by this point I have been in a personal relationship with God for almost three years. As with any relationship you learn how to speak to each other and with God it is no different. When you start to seek Him out and actually become aware that he wants a part of every aspect of your life He will speak to you. Sometimes it's gentle, sometimes if needed, it's louder than lightning. This day was a lightning day and the subject for discussion was bankruptcy.

By now you've read a few stories about how messed up I was financially. It all came to a head when a few people suggested that I think about filing bankruptcy and starting over. I had brought a lot of personal debt when I opened my business and then racked up a lot of credit card debt with the start-up.

I got in over my head and then with the economy crashing things got a little scary. I just wanted out of everything. I have always had a decent amount of debt, but never like this before. I also, always had a steady job, so my debt was very manageable. I was able to do pretty much whatever I wanted whenever I wanted, but I wasn't loaded by any means. Let's just chalk it up to poor money management.

I definitely was not practicing anything biblical in the financial area, but I wanted to get to that place now. Here I was facing a huge decision and my past was coming back to haunt me. I had come so far on my Christian journey that it upset me that I still was cleaning up so many messes. I was so tired of dealing with it that I wanted to give up. Maybe bankruptcy was the right thing for me.

I got up the nerve to call a Christian bankruptcy attorney. After speaking to one of my friends she gave me some advice and just said very compassionately that I needed to face reality and just make the call.

She thought I would only know what God wanted me to do if I faced my fear and my reality. I could not ignore it any longer. With a deep breath and an anxious heart I dialed the number. The lawyer told me the paperwork to bring on Monday and went over the process briefly.

"Do you have any assets?"

"Yes, my car is paid off."

"How much is it worth?"

"About $8000 I think."

"The judge may want to take your car and put that toward your case."

My heart sank and my eyes began to tear up. I don't remember what else was said, because it didn't matter. I was not going to give up my car that I worked hard for five years to pay off. I was angry, but I didn't let her know. I just said "okay, I'll get everything together and see you on Monday."

My facial room was my safe place so I locked the door and went back to my room and just cried. I couldn't believe that I let myself get into this situation. The only thing I had left was my business. The one thing that was mine that was still here. My identity was my business. Dad was gone. Josh was gone. Now this was being threatened. What else do I have to lose?

"I'm so sorry God, I made such a mess of things and was so careless with all you trusted me with, I need you. Please forgive me and show me what I need to do."

I pulled myself together as much as possible and left early since no one was coming in the rest of the afternoon. Sammy and I went for a little walk and Daisee and Duke were settled. My eyes weren't puffy anymore so I went to the gym at my church to clear my head. After my work-out on the way out I met Carl who works there part-time and we started chatting.

"You work out on Friday night usually?" Carl asked.

"I have my own business and always have to work Saturday mornings so Fridays are good for me."

Carl mentioned that he had owned his own business years ago, but unfortunately had to file bankruptcy. We struck up a conversation and he opened up pretty quickly about the struggles he had with running his own business.

In the middle of him telling me the story he said "I'm not sure why I'm telling you all this personal information."

"It's okay, I have that effect on people and I do it to. Can I ask you question though? How long did the process take?"

"About three months I think."

"Okay, one more question, when you got the phone call that it was all done, how did you feel?"

"Relieved, I think I actually got sleep that night." Thinking of all the sleepless nights I had and creditors calling me 20+ times a day my eyes began to well up.

"I may have to make that decision soon. It's been really hard recently."

Carl said that he regretted his decision and didn't want me to have to go through that. At this point I was standing at the desk across from him and he could see the burden in my eyes. He said gently, "Angie, my advice would be to do everything you can to avoid this."

I knew right then that God was speaking directly through Carl. There's my answer. "Can I pray for you?" he asked.

"Yes, that would be nice, thank you." He grabbed my hands and held them and he prayed for me. I don't remember exactly what was said, but I felt the Holy Spirit moving. At this point I had never experienced someone praying for me who I had just met. I had been in a Bible study so I was used to praying in a group but not at the gym with someone I literally just met? I was in awe of how God worked. That night he spoke right through Carl and calmed my spirit through a simple prayer.

I see Carl at church and at the gym from time to time and he always asks about my business. I can only hope that by his story being in this book that he realizes how God used him in a big way in my life. I tell Carl how that conversation saved me. My business is growing and I'm halfway out of debt.

I never filed bankruptcy. When I left that night I felt in my heart that I hadn't tried my best to avoid it. On the drive home I asked God to give me the wisdom to get out of my mess and I told him I didn't want to give up.

What I learned about God: He won't give up on you and He speaks through other people

I hope that we can all learn to be transparent with each other and understand that by sharing our struggles we can help someone else. You may never know when the opportunity will arise. Maybe God will use your situation to speak into someone else's life someday. He will help you get through it and come out victorious on the other side so that you can be a blessing too.

I was so exhausted that day. I felt like a complete failure and I had no hope left. I didn't know if I had it in me to keep going. I was glad that God worked it out that I made the phone call to the attorney on Thursday and I couldn't get an appointment until Monday. He gave me time to process everything and settle down so that I could hear from Him. God knew exactly what I needed to hear to give me hope again and He chose Carl to deliver the message. From that day forward I never looked back. It hasn't been easy but it was what I needed to hear at the right moment to get back up again.

Thank you Carl, for sharing your struggle with me and for praying with me, God used your trial to help me in my time of need.

Matthew 18:19 (NIV) *¹⁹ "Again, truly I tell you that if two of you on earth agree about anything they ask for, it will be done for them by my Father in heaven.*

BOOK 6- THE FIRST TIME I HEARD GOD'S VOICE SO CLEARLY

I was still attending Southeast and was getting connected with other women on the same journey through a Bible study. I had never done this before but I really enjoyed the fellowship and it helped me to start reading God's word. I wasn't sure why I had never read the Bible. It was all new to me and I thought that was strange given the fact that I went to Catholic schools for 13 years.

I attended the Christmas Joy program at my church in Dec.'09 with some of the ladies I met at church. The speaker was Kristen Sauder. I didn't know anything about her except she had written a Bible study and was a member at SECC.

Her topic was "Ordinary Mary" and she spoke about how Mary must have been so overwhelmed at the call placed on her from God. Mary was just an ordinary girl that was chosen by God to do something extraordinary. Imagine how she felt in the presence of the angel Gabriel who was sent to deliver her this message. Mary said yes to God and was obedient even though she might face opposition, after-all she was still a virgin and she would have to tell her fiancé that she was going to have a child. Kristen was challenging us to put ourselves in Mary's shoes. Would we say yes to God if he asked something of us? Or would we ignore Him or the call placed on our lives?

One thing she said that really has changed my life and I so believe was a direct message to me from God was when she told a story about her own disobedience. She said (and I am going by memory) that she was sitting in church during a service and I think it was during communion and she heard God clearly ask her to go to up to the bottom of the steps and get down on her knees and pray. She said she had a discussion quietly in her thoughts with God and simply said "we don't do that here God" – and no one else was doing it, so she didn't do it. She remembers how strongly she felt Him and what He was asking her to do.

I thought she was going to say that something amazing happened but she was honest enough to tell the truth and admit that she didn't do what God asked her to do. She said she regrets so much saying no to Him that day because she will never know what God wanted from her and what could have happened had she simply obeyed and said yes.

Well, I didn't realize that shortly after that program I would hear God's voice so clearly for the first time when I was doing dishes at my sister's house.

Michelle was going through a very rough patch in her life when I was living with her. I moved out of my brother's rental property and into Michelle's walk-out basement because it was cheaper and it would help her out too. We were both pretty strapped financially so we thought it made more sense.

Well this night she was pretty sad and she was in her bedroom asleep or trying to get to sleep. I was standing at the kitchen sink doing dishes when I heard the clearest voice in my ear saying, "Go pray with her."

I literally said out loud –

"What?"

"Do you mean: go pray FOR her?"

"Go pray with her." He said again.

Are you kidding me? I've never prayed in front of anyone much less my sister Michelle who I have a love/hate relationship with and tonight was not the night to be bothering her with a prayer. What am I going to say? What is she going to say? Is she going to make fun of me? Is she going to get mad at me and kick me out of the room? All of these thoughts happened in about 2 minutes.

I went to the stairway down to the walk out basement and I had a short conversation with God.

"God, are you for real? You want me to go pray with her? Can't I just say a prayer for her, quietly?"

It was as if I could hear him saying "Do what I am telling you to do, I will help you."

"Okay I will do this but you have to give me the words to say because I have no idea what I am doing?"

I walked back up the stairs. If anyone would have seen me pacing back and forth and talking to God they would have thrown me in the loony bin.

I remembered Kristen's story and how she felt not knowing what God wanted from her that day. I knew I had to obey so I went to her door and knocked quietly.

"Michelle, you still up? "

"Yes"

"I need to tell you something." I turned the light on. "Uh, I am a little nervous to tell you this."

"What is it?"

"God just told me to come pray with you!"

"Are you for real?"

I thought to myself – that's what I just said.

"I've never done this before but I have to do it and just bear with me because I'm shaking —Can I pray with you?"

She said yes. So I went and sat down next to her on her bed. I was so nervous. What in the world was I going to say?

She looked at me with her sad eyes and said, "Aren't we supposed to hold hands or something?"

We both started laughing but we knew it was serious. So I said okay – and I started praying out loud and the prayer went on for a while but the Holy Spirit gave me the right words to pray.

It was a beautiful moment, Michelle had tears in her eyes and we both said amen and that was that. She said thank you.

I cannot describe the feeling of doing that that night. I am so thankful for Kristen's story of obedience. Sometimes all we need to do to help other people that we care about is to just pray for them. We may not have the right words but God knows what we need to pray for.

When God tells you or places on your heart to pray for someone or to do something...don't wait and let the opportunity pass you by. You could be saving a life eternally just by planting a small seed. Just trust in God and that He knows what He is doing. Even if it looks impossible or if other people may look at you funny. Just do it!

What I learned about God: Don't be afraid to do something that you know God is telling you to do

Sometimes God will stretch you and ask you to do some crazy things. Each time he has asked me to do something and I did it, it always gave me peace in the end. I was nervous before I would do it but then I would just say "ok, let's do it God" and go for it. I may not know exactly what the reason was for Him asking me but the whole point is that I trusted Him to take care of me when I was obedient. Trust me when I tell you that He has asked me to do some things lately that have been way out of my comfort zone, including writing this book. I may not even see the results of what He has called me to do for a very long time. It's all about trust. He knows what He is doing!

Proverbs 3:5 (NIV)

Trust in the LORD with all your heart and lean not on your own understanding;

BOOK 7- GOD IS ENOUGH

It was Kentucky Derby time in Louisville and the kick-off event *Thunder over Louisville* is two weeks before. It's a massive fireworks display. Downtown Louisville lights up and thousands and thousands of people line the banks of the Ohio River to watch. I have always loved fireworks since I was little and have such fond memories of celebrations that included them. My family used to go to King's Island amusement park right outside of Cincinnatti, Ohio, in the summers growing up. The day always ended with a grand fireworks display. As a kid and even young adult this was my favorite part of the day other than a few roller-coasters and the pizza and ice cream. The days were long and we had about an hour and half drive home but we stayed for the fireworks most of the time.

My boyfriend and I got to spend one "Thunder" together in 2008 and it was so much fun. We spent the whole day together and stayed until the bitter end. I was so excited to have someone to go with me. There's something romantic about sharing a sprawled out blanket under the stars and a beautiful display of lights in the night sky.

This particular "Thunder" night in 2011 was a rainy one. It poured down rain all day and I didn't really want to go out in the mess. It also reminded me of the last time I went with Josh and made me really sad. I felt alone and the fact that I didn't have anyone to go with was depressing. I was definitely having a small pity party for awhile so I took a break from myself and took Sammy out to go potty. I could hear the fireworks in the distance since I was a little closer to the river in my new apartment. It just made it worse because I wanted to see them and couldn't.

Talk about pathetic. I was by myself again on a Saturday night. I wondered when or if I would meet someone again.

I was technically ok being single at this point. I had accepted losing Josh and I thought I was ready to meet someone but I had the sense in my heart that God wanted me to Himself for a little longer. I don't remember ever being fully content about being single but I was certainly ok being by myself. I knew that it would happen when it was supposed to happen but I started to get the feeling that my timing was way off from God's. Doesn't it say somewhere in the Bible that with God a day is like a thousand years and a thousand years is like a day? I was praying that God's version of soon was the same as mine this time around.

Maybe I wasn't supposed to get married. The doubt crept in a little. I didn't want to accept that thought because I knew that God had placed that desire in my heart. I just had to hang in there and have faith.

I was a little frustrated with God sometimes though. Didn't I suffer enough? My hopes were shattered but not by a break up. It was a death! I never in my wildest dreams imagined that I would have to go through that kind of pain. I do remember praying to God that I would rather know what it was like to love and lose then never to love at all. It wasn't long before I met Josh that I prayed that. After he died my hope was destroyed. Who was I without him? I put the weight of the world on his shoulders. I expected him to complete me. I missed him so much but I had a profound realization that night that I was his girlfriend longer than I actually knew him. We only knew each other for seven months but I was his girlfriend for three years and had just recently accepted the fact that I had to let him go. I was finally in a place of contentment. It was just me and God.

All of this was racing through my mind as I sat by myself in my bedroom. I guess I wasn't by myself, I had Sammy, Duke and Daisee right there beside me and they were happy that I was home.

I couldn't help but drift back in thought to my old life. Wow, things have changed. When I moved home my dreams were coming true and now all those plans of finding love failed. I picked up a Bible study I was doing but I wasn't real happy about doing it right at that moment. I wrestled with watching TV but something inside felt like I was supposed to be doing this study. It was quiet, no music, no TV just me and God on a Saturday night. "Shouldn't I be happier doing this?" I thought.

I missed my old life. "Is this it?" I wondered if God wanted me to give up everything I loved to be with Him. In the Bible it speaks about losing your life to live and so on but I guess I never took that literally. It's not like I didn't want to spend time with God but on a Saturday night? Thunder?

I reminisced about the days where my life was full of plans to go to this party or that event. When I would say "Sorry I already have plans, can I take a rain-check?" I never stopped to even think about God except for on Sundays when I would go to church and that was not even all the time. God wasn't in my life everyday or in every decision or plan I made. He was there when I needed Him or when I wanted something. He was there when someone I loved was in the hospital or when I didn't have any idea how I was going to pay a bill.

I stopped fussing and opened my Bible study. I don't

remember which one I was doing but it was my first one I did on my own since I had just left my study group. I started feeling God pull me away from everyone including my study group and tonight was just a confirmation that he was wiping out my social calendar to work on our relationship. So I kept on reading. As I read, the thoughts of emptiness began to wear off and I started thinking about my life and how full it had become recently. Don't get me wrong, I am still a social person but it's just different now. I don't feel the need to go out and get drunk anymore. It doesn't satisfy me. It only ended in headache and heartache anyways so I'm not missing out on anything by not having that in my life anymore. I don't get invited to a lot of parties nowadays but I've learned to accept that too. I think people don't know what to do with you when you quit drinking. I also realized that I had peace in my life. There was no more chaos, no more drama and that was nice. I really was satisfied and content. I was happy to be home, cozy and dry, with my babies right next to me.

It was very peaceful in my house that night and I started talking out loud to God which is normal for me, I told Him I was sorry for complaining about being single and being by myself all the time. I told Him that even though I sometimes miss my old life I wouldn't trade it for my relationship with Him. I felt I was content for the first time in my life. I do, of course, want to meet the person He has planned for me but I am willing to wait. I want to experience the blessings from God in my next relationship. When I lost Josh, I lost hope and now I'm being given a second chance at love, to do it God's way.

I expressed how much love I had for Josh and that I was so thankful that he was in my life. I was ready though, after three years, to meet someone.

Deep down I really was finally enjoying my alone time with God. I was just so used to complaining about being by myself. Plus, society makes you feel like you have to be with someone to be happy so I bought right into it. I know plenty of people that are with the wrong person and they know it but are scared to wait for the right one. I knew God didn't want me to do that anymore.

In my moment of asking for forgiveness I could hear Him say "Our time is coming to an end." I knew what He meant by that. It was like my heart knew exactly what He was saying without skipping a beat. I thought that it would make me happy to hear that but it made me sad. Here I was, after all this time, acknowledging, accepting and even enjoying being with God alone and now He tells me that my husband is right around the corner. He didn't have to say it, my heart knew it. I knew that it didn't mean that my special relationship with Him was going to be over just because I would have a partner in my life. It just meant that I would have to work at it a little harder, finding that quiet time and just being with God. Now, I have that all the time but things would be changing soon. I had built a friendship with God and I could find Him anytime I needed and I could talk to Him freely and out loud whenever I wanted. There's a freedom in that and now I found myself not sure if I wanted that to change. That night I felt humbled that God, even after all my complaining and all the mistakes I made, still wanted to bless me with someone to love.

In the still of the night, all alone, God gave me hope again.

What I learned about God: His love never changes and he is always faithful

I have come to understand that God's love is above all the rest. To have a relationship with Jesus is the ultimate love and there's only one way to find out what that feels like, you have to spend time with Him and seek Him. I never understood what "falling in love with Jesus" meant. I would hear people say that when they found Jesus their lives got changed and I just didn't get it. It is hard to comprehend but it is true. We can't all be crazy, right?

I have now changed my priorities when it comes to my next relationship. I will put God first, then my husband. My whole life has been spent giving God the leftovers and doing things backwards. I want to experience the blessing of having God at the center. I know it doesn't mean life will be perfect but to have a spiritually strong marriage is something I look forward to. I believe God has a great guy planned for me so I just have to have faith that his timing is perfect.

Of course, I am hoping that it will be before I am 80!!!

Thankfully God has a sense of humor too!

Romans 8:38-39 (NIV)

[38] *For I am convinced that neither death nor life, neither angels nor demons,*[a] *neither the present nor the future, nor any powers,* [39] *neither height nor depth, nor anything else in all creation, will be able to separate us from the love of God that is in Christ Jesus our Lord.*

GOD IS STILL WRITING OUR STORY

He Continues to Give Hope

I have to admit that writing my story has been one of the most challenging things I have ever done. Every emotion has been brought to the surface many times. Yet it was good to work through and let go of the hurts and disappointments, the mistakes and failures, the guilt and anger, and focus on what has come out of all of it.

Sometimes as I would read over what I had written it was hard to see myself as that person on the pages. I don't recognize her anymore. It was only five years ago this year that I moved back home from Orlando to Louisville and only four years that my world came crashing down. In that brief amount of time, which seemed like eternity, I experienced great loss, learned some major life lessons, faced my biggest fears and had my life completely turned around.

One of the primary lessons I learned is that as soon as

you accept Christ in your heart, your past is no longer your story, the future is. That's why it was occasionally difficult to tell this story and believe it was ever my life. I still wonder why God wanted me to open my heart to complete strangers and put it down in ink for eternity. Truthfully, I don't know and I may never know. I just had to do what He told me to do and trust that He is going to work it out to His glory.

I wish I could report that everything is absolutely perfect and that I have fallen in love, wiped out all my debt and am now bringing home a huge salary.

I can't do that because God is still writing my story.

I can tell you, however, that I have more hope for my future than ever before. My business is doing great. I am paying down my debt and learning to listen to God's instruction in EVERY area of my life. It's such a peaceful feeling knowing that God has got me. I still try to take control from time to time when I feel like He is not moving quick enough but He gently reminds me that He is in control. I don't have to be struck by lightning now for Him to get His point across.

Well, maybe sometimes.

I think one of the main things I have had lifted off of me is guilt. In the beginning of my journey with God I used to think that every time I messed up He was going to wipe out everything and punish me. I came to understand the difference between discipline and punishment. God disciplines as a loving father does because He loves us. He loves me and He loves YOU. He wants us to repent of our sins, ask for forgiveness and not do those things anymore. Of course we are going to mess up from time to time but the closer you get to God the less likely you'll want to continue doing the wrong things. It's just how it works.

It's all about being forgiven and accepting that forgiveness from God. It's also about forgiving others as well, just as God has forgiven us.

God wants to write your story too but you have to let go of the reins. The more you resist the longer it will take to find your purpose, what God has called you to do. He has called ALL of us to do something for Him, for His glory, but you have to obediently focus on God so that He can reveal His plan for you. I promise you that once you do He will give you more than you can ask or imagine. The joy that comes when you have Jesus in your heart is indescribable. If I feel like this now, without having all the earthly things I used to seek, I can only imagine how it will feel when I receive the many gifts God has in store for me but hasn't yet revealed.

Every so often, when I get a little down or restless, God speaks to me and reminds me that He is here, just like He always has been. I take a deep breath, close my eyes, think about my cross in the sky and open my eyes again.

"I know." I say with a sigh and a slight smile. "I know you've got me God."

I will hold onto the HOPE that God has given me, press forward and pray that you can do the same. I know that many of you reading this may have suffered great trials and may have no idea how you are ever going to get through it. You don't have to stay in that place. God doesn't want you there. He wants you to feel alive again. He wants you to be free. This may sound hokey to some but I am telling you from personal experience it is the truth and the truth shall set you free.

My prayer is that you will make a decision for hope and realize its importance in your faith walk with Christ. It's up to you. God is waiting for you!

Trust in Christ, He will give you the strength to get through it.

Grace and love,

Angie

Lamentations 3:25 (NIV)

[25] *The LORD is good to those whose hope is in him, to the one who seeks him.*

A Call to Action

My prayer is that you have seen how God is a God of Hope and that He can heal all wounds. The most important thing I can think of to get you on the right track is to find a Bible and a Bible preaching church in your area and start getting connected with people who have been down a similar path. We don't all have the same struggles but they are usually similar and we must use our trials to help other people.

I can't tell you how important it is to have encouraging friends in your life, ones that will speak God's truth into your life when others won't. It's so easy to get down and out and start doubting yourself when the people around you don't have faith in Christ. It's just different when you have another believer by your side to walk alongside you. He or she can build you up as well as point out when you are listening to lies instead of truth. Only a strong believer will be able to stand firm with you on your journey. It doesn't mean you have to live in a Christian bubble either. Just be choosy on who you get your advice from. Let your light shine to those around you who may not know God's love so that they will want what you have. You don't have to become a coo-coo Christian to get your point across. Trust me, that won't win them over. Once you have Christ in your heart He will do that for you. He is the only one who can save a lost soul. It is not you or me but He does work through us.

One more thing I recommend is that you try to listen to some Christian music on the radio. If you give it a chance I promise you it can change your life.

Trust in Jesus and make Him your Lord and Savior and you will be SAVED!!

Romans 15:13(NIV)

[13] *May the God of hope fill you with all joy and peace as you trust in him, so that you may overflow with hope by the power of the Holy Spirit.*